TIME
FOR KIDS
READERS

CARRIE CHAPMAN CATT

by Betsy Ochester

Harcourt

Orlando   Austin   Chicago   New York   Toronto   London   San Diego

Visit *The Learning Site!*
www.harcourtschool.com

VO FOR PRESIDENT.

HORACE GREELEY OF NEW YORK

A Shocking Idea

Thirteen-year-old Carrie Lane would remember Election Day in 1872 for the rest of her life.

For weeks, the Lanes had been talking about the upcoming presidential election. Carrie knew her mother and father favored the candidate Horace Greeley. Greeley, a famous newspaper editor, was running against United States President Ulysses S. Grant. Grant was a national hero. He had been the North's top military commander during the Civil War (1861–1865).

On Election Day, Carrie's father and a man who worked for him put on good clothes to go into town to vote. Carrie asked her mother why she wasn't changing her clothes, too. "I'm not going," her mother replied.

"Then how are you going to vote for Mr. Greeley?" Carrie asked.

The whole family laughed at Carrie's question. At that time in the United States, only men were allowed to vote in national elections.

Soon afterwards, a neighbor boy came to visit Carrie. She said to him, "I think it's unfair that women can't vote, don't you?" The neighbor laughed at Carrie, too.

"What's so funny about women voting?" Carrie demanded.

"Well," the boy replied, "naturally they can't vote."

Carrie didn't think this was natural at all. She thought that not allowing women to vote was a ridiculous idea. At 13, Carrie believed strongly that women should have the same rights as men. She became determined to do something about it. As an adult, she would lead the successful campaign to win voting rights for all women in the United States.

ULYSSES S. GRANT

FROM FARM TO PODIUM

Carrie Clinton Lane was born in Ripon, Wisconsin, on January 9, 1859. When she was seven years old, the family moved to a farm in Charles City, Iowa.

Carrie was independent, curious, and intelligent. When she graduated from high school, she wanted to attend college. Her father viewed college as an unnecessary luxury for a daughter. At that time few girls went to college. Since her father knew that Carrie would not change her mind, he offered to pay $25 a year toward college. The tuition was $150 per year. Carrie would have to earn the rest.

Carrie had already made plans to do just that. She taught school for a year and saved money for college. She entered Iowa Agricultural College (now Iowa State University) in 1877. Part-time jobs helped her pay her bills. She washed dishes for 9 cents an hour and worked in the library for 10 cents an hour.

At college, Carrie discovered she had a talent for giving powerful speeches. During her first year at Iowa State, Carrie, then 18 years old, spoke

Ripon, Wisconsin, about 1860.

at a school for teachers. In her speech, she talked about women's suffrage, or the right to vote. *Suffrage* comes from the Latin word for "to vote for," or "to support." Suffragists, women and men fighting for women's right to vote, often wrote "woman suffrage" or "women suffrage" instead of "women's suffrage."

In her speech, Carrie disputed the common claim that women were not intelligent enough to vote. "How is it possible," Carrie asked, "that a woman who is unfit to vote should be the mother of, and bring up, a man who is?" Carrie's speech caused enough stir to be reported in her hometown newspaper.

It took Carrie Lane just three years to finish college. She graduated in 1880 at the head of her class. Energetic, bright, and ambitious, Carrie had her heart set on making things better for the women of the world.

**Carrie Chapman Catt
1859–1947**

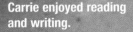
Carrie enjoyed reading and writing.

Becoming a lawyer seemed to be a good place to start. Carrie went to work in a lawyer's office in Charles City, Iowa. Soon an offer came to teach high school in Mason City, Iowa. The job would pay $40 a month. She took it, planning to earn enough money to go to law school.

Carrie enjoyed teaching. She was well liked and respected by students and fellow teachers. Within a year, she had decided not to go to law school. In her second year in Mason City, Carrie was appointed the city's superintendent of schools. She became one of the first women in the nation to head an entire city's school system.

During this time, Carrie met a young newspaper publisher and editor named Leo Chapman. When the two married in 1885, Carrie—now known as Carrie Chapman—had to resign from her teaching and administrative duties. Married women were not allowed to teach.

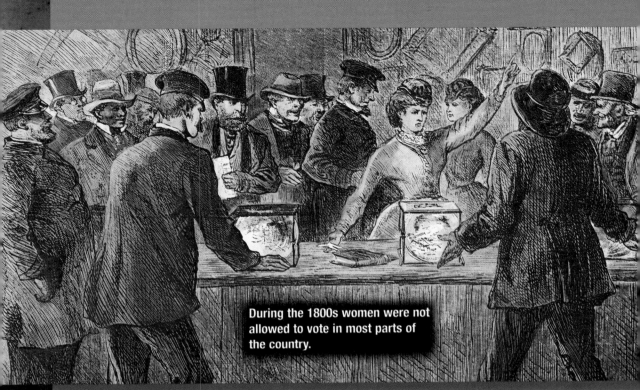

During the 1800s women were not allowed to vote in most parts of the country.

Carrie worked with her new husband on his newspaper, the *Mason City Republican*. She wrote a weekly column called "Woman's World." In it, she discussed economic and political issues. A year later, Leo and Carrie decided to sell the newspaper and leave Mason City. They planned to move to San Francisco. Leo went west first, in May 1886, while Carrie visited with her family in Charles City. She planned to join Leo when he was settled. In August, she received an urgent telegram. Leo was sick with typhoid fever, a deadly disease. Carrie left for California on the next train. By the time she arrived, Leo was dead.

Heartbroken, Carrie decided to remain in San Francisco. She spent a year there, staying with an aunt and working as a journalist. Carrie was San Francisco's first female newspaper reporter. She continued to improve her skills as a public speaker. In 1887 Carrie returned to Charles City and to a new career. She joined the Iowa Woman Suffrage Association, as a professional lecturer and organizer.

THE SUFFRAGE MOVEMENT

Americans had begun the struggle for a woman's right to vote before Carrie was born. In 1848, Lucretia Mott and Elizabeth Cady Stanton organized the nation's first women's rights convention. Hundreds of people went to the two-day meeting in Seneca Falls, New York. There they drafted a Declaration of Sentiments, or opinions.

The document was a surprise to a lot of people. It was inspired by the Declaration of Independence, which says that "all men are created equal." The Declaration of Sentiments said that "all men and women are created equal." It also demanded the right of women to keep wages they earned and to own property. At the time, women could do neither. The document also demanded the right to vote.

Susan B. Anthony was another early leader of the women's suffrage movement. She teamed up with Elizabeth Cady Stanton and helped

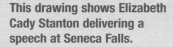

This drawing shows Elizabeth Cady Stanton delivering a speech at Seneca Falls.

the suffrage movement form a single united group, the National American Woman Suffrage Association (NAWSA).

NAWSA held its first public meeting in 1890. Among the speakers was an impressive delegate from Iowa named Carrie Chapman. Susan B. Anthony was looking for young talent for the national suffrage movement. Carrie caught her eye. In 1892 she asked Carrie to address the United States Congress on women's suffrage. She also made Carrie responsible for recruiting and educating suffragists nationwide.

This cartoon shows Susan B. Anthony in patriotic clothing.

9

San Francisco was one of the largest cities on the West Coast when Carrie traveled there in 1887.

LEADER OF THE CAUSE

As Carrie embarked on her new career, she found a new supporter. While in San Francisco in 1887, she had run into an old college friend from Ames, Iowa, George Catt. The two fell in love. They married in 1890.

George believed in women's suffrage. When he and Carrie married, they agreed that she could devote four months each year to suffrage work. George's job as an engineer took the Catts to Seattle and then to New York City, where they settled.

In 1900 Susan B. Anthony stepped down as president of NAWSA. The group's delegates chose Carrie to be their next president. Carrie quickly brought every state and national territory into NAWSA. She also drew wealthy women to the cause. This helped bring needed money into the organization.

Carrie believed that women and men in every country should have equal rights. So shortly after becoming president of NAWSA, she founded the International Woman Suffrage Alliance (IWSA). Today the organization is called the International Alliance of Women.

In 1904 George Catt fell ill. Carrie resigned from her job as NAWSA president to care for him. George died in October 1905. During the next two years, Carrie also lost her brother William, her mother, and her adviser and friend Susan B. Anthony. Her grief was so deep, it affected her health. Her doctor and friends encouraged her to travel. She took their advice and spent most of the next eight years in other countries around the world.

Carrie promoted women's rights throughout Africa, Europe, and Asia. She urged women everywhere to join IWSA. "The cause we represent," she said, "belongs to no country and no nation or race, but is a common demand of our united womanhood."

Carrie took the cause of suffrage to other countries where women were fighting hard for the right to vote.

Women at an information booth in New York City encourage people to support women's suffrage.

During long periods at home, she continued to work for NAWSA. One task she took was the battle to win the right to vote for women in New York. States had the power to let women vote in local and state elections. By 1912 ten states had given women that right.

Carrie could not convince New York lawmakers to give women the vote. However, her leadership skills made her even more famous. She was at the front of the national women's movement once more.

Why did New York lawmakers oppose giving women the right to vote? For the same reasons that some people did throughout the nation. Some argued that the right to vote would cause trouble for women and their families.

Some people against women's suffrage claimed that political discussions between husbands and wives would lead to divorce. Others said that voting was "unwomanly." One male politician said, "I honor women too highly to allow them to descend into the dirty pool of politics." Some even said women were not smart enough to vote or that they didn't want to vote. Of course, the millions of women fighting for suffrage proved them wrong.

THE WOMAN'S HOUR

In 1915 Carrie again became NAWSA's president. The organization now had more than two million members. Carrie faced a difficult situation. NAWSA's previous leaders had let it become weak and divided. The group had lost its direction. It had no plan to achieve its goals.

Carrie knew NAWSA was going through a crisis. She believed that with a strong, organized push, women could win the right to vote. "The time has come," she said in 1916, "to shout . . . in tones so clear and jubilant that they will . . . echo from shore to shore: 'The woman's Hour has struck!'" The time was right, she believed, for suffragists to make a final push.

Carrie unveiled what she called her "Winning Plan" at a meeting of NAWSA members in 1916. First, she reminded her listeners of their goal—to get lawmakers to pass an amendment, or addition, to the United States Constitution. The amendment was very simple. It had been written in the 1870s. "The right of citizens of the United States to vote," it says in part, "shall not be denied or abridged [narrowed] by the United States or by any state on account of sex."

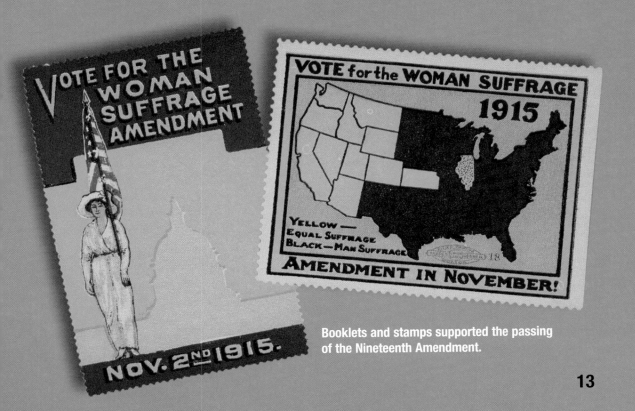

Booklets and stamps supported the passing of the Nineteenth Amendment.

Getting the amendment passed would require
action at two levels—in individual states and in
Washington, D.C. To win passage of the amendment,
Carrie said, NAWSA first had to get state lawmakers
on its side. It had to persuade the lawmakers to grant
women the vote in state and local elections.

Suffragists picket President Woodrow Wilson outside the White House gates in January 1917. They hoped to get him to support the passing of the Nineteenth Amendment.

NAWSA opened an office in Washington, D.C. They worked hard to convince members of Congress to focus on adding a women's suffrage amendment to the United States Constitution. Carrie even tried to get U.S. President Woodrow Wilson to think about it, but his mind was on other things. World War I (1914–1918) was raging in Europe.

These women factory workers are assembling military vehicles during World War I.

The United States entered the war in April 1917. Carrie urged suffragists to continue to work for voting rights while supporting the nation's war efforts.

Even before United States soldiers were sent to Europe, suffragists were arguing over how to reach their goals. One group, the National Women's Party (NWP), was led by a social worker named Alice Paul. Paul blamed President Wilson's party, the Democrats, for keeping women from winning the vote. In 1916 she spoke to women who could vote in their state elections. She asked them to vote against Democratic candidates for state office.

Alice Paul (1885–1977)

Carrie didn't like Alice Paul's plan. Many Democrats supported women's suffrage, and Carrie did not want to anger them. She knew that NAWSA had friends and enemies in both the Democratic and Republican parties.

After the United States entered World War I, NWP members held protests in front of the White House. The signs they carried demanded action on women's suffrage. Some of the protesters even chained themselves to a White House fence to get attention for their cause. Paul's tactics kept the issue on the front pages of newspapers. Despite the objections of some, support for women's suffrage grew.

The work women did during the war changed a lot of people's minds about women's suffrage. Women became an important part of the war effort. They worked in weapons factories, in steel mills, and at other jobs once held only by men. Women raised money for the war effort and did countless other things to serve their country. Because of this, many people thought that women could no longer be denied the right to vote.

Carrie (center) attended a political rally in favor of women's suffrage with the wife of the governor of New York (left) and the chairperson of the New York State Suffrage Party.

THE WINNING PLAN

Around this time, the Winning Plan that Carrie had unveiled in 1916 began to take hold. NAWSA gained strength and direction. In 1917 six more states passed laws that gave women the right to vote in state elections. One of the states was New York.

New York had the largest population of any state and the most representatives in the U.S. Congress. The law allowing women to vote in New York elections gave the suffragist movement a big boost. The time was right, Carrie decided, for women to win the vote in national elections. Again, she urged President Wilson to support her cause. This time, he said he would.

On January 10, 1918, the U.S. House of Representatives scheduled a vote on a proposal to change the Constitution to guarantee women's suffrage. The house galleries were packed with excited suffragists and anti-suffragists.

The suffragists had asked all their friends in the House for support. Three representatives left their hospital beds to vote. Another was carried in on a stretcher. One representative's wife, a loyal suffragist, was dying. She insisted he leave her bedside to vote.

In the end, the House voted to amend the Constitution and guarantee women's right to vote. The suffragists cheered. But nearly a year and a half passed before the Senate approved the amendment, on June 4, 1919.

Before the amendment could become law, there was still another step—it was a big one. Lawmakers in 36 of the 48 states had to approve the amendment. Would there be enough state support to do that?

Less than an hour after the final Senate vote, Carrie sent telegrams to state governors. The telegrams urged the governors to have their legislatures meet in special sessions. Many did so. Within four months, 17 states had approved the amendment. Nineteen more were needed.

For a while, it looked as if the lawmakers in several western states would oppose the amendment. Carrie traveled west to promote it. She called her trip the Wake Up America tour. She and other leading suffragists gave speeches and held meetings with governors and state officials.

The suffragists' hard work paid off. By the spring of 1920, 35 states had approved the amendment. Only one more state was needed.

Carrie (seated in the center at the back of the car) takes part in a parade in New York that celebrates the approval of the Nineteenth Amendment.

A Mother's Wish

Suffragists knew that Tennessee was their best bet. Carrie packed an overnight bag and went to Nashville, the state capital. She thought she would be there for two or three days. She stayed for two months. Persuading Tennessee lawmakers to pass the amendment was one of the toughest battles she had ever faced.

Opponents of the amendment had traveled to Tennessee. Carrie stayed to fight them. She toured the state to rally support for the amendment. She got local women's groups behind the amendment and asked state lawmakers to vote for it.

On August 13, 1920, the Tennessee Senate passed the amendment. But the real battle was in Tennessee's House of Representatives. Representatives for and against the amendment were almost evenly numbered.

On August 18, the chamber in which the representatives met was packed with spectators. The representatives voted twice, and each time the outcome was a tie. On the third vote, Harry Burn broke the tie. At 24 years old, he was the state's youngest representative. When his name was called, he shouted, "Yea!"

Three-quarters of the states had approved the Nineteenth Amendment. It was now a law. Supporters of the amendment cheered wildly. Foes booed or just hung their heads. Several of them chased Burn around the room. He escaped to the capitol's attic and hid there for the rest of the day.

The Nineteenth Amendment is only 39 words long, but those 39 words changed the nation. The amendment reads:
"The right of citizens of the United States to vote shall not be denied or abridged by the United States or by any state on account of sex. Congress shall have power to enforce this article by appropriate legislation."

Women's right to vote is now part of the Constitution of the United States of America.

The next day, Burn was asked to explain why he had changed his mind. He pulled a telegram out of his pocket. It was from his mother. "Don't forget to be a good boy," she wrote, "and help Mrs. Catt." He did, and he made history.

Shortly before the Nineteenth Amendment became law, Carrie reorganized NAWSA into the League of Women Voters. Now that women could vote, she figured, they needed to learn how to make their votes count. The League would teach them.

Carrie Chapman Catt is best known for her leadership role in getting the Nineteenth Amendment passed. But she never stopped trying to make the world a better place. For the rest of her life, she continued to travel around the country and the world. Wherever she went, she promoted women's rights and world peace.

Peace was the issue Carrie cared most about after 1920. In 1925 she founded the National Committee on the Cause and Cure of War. She supported the League of Nations, which set the stage for today's United Nations. She also worked to win support for the United Nations, which was founded in 1945.

Two years later, on March 9, 1947, Carrie Chapman Catt died of heart failure at her home in New Rochelle, New York. She was 88 years old. Seventy-five years earlier, she had dreamed of a fairer world. By the time she died, she had helped that dream come true.

This portrait of Carrie Chapman Catt was painted by Mary Foote in 1927.

Tough Talk

In 1999 a group made up of 137 professors chose the best 100 political speeches of the twentieth century. A speech Carrie Chapman Catt made in 1916 was on the list. Here are examples of words she used to inspire her listeners:

"We women demand an equal voice; we shall accept nothing less." (1911)

"The veins of American women are not filled with milk and water. They are neither cowards nor slackers. They will come [to join the struggle for women's suffrage]. They only await the bugle call to learn that the final battle is on." (1916)